CU00536033

First published in 2022

978-1-4478-9190-1
Imprint: Lulu.com

The Lifting

POEMS

MICHAEL MAY

FOR
MARIAN

Contents

Amoebae 1
Anthology 2
This is the day 8
Lotissement 10
Ballyhornan 11
I was sad in my lacking to reach you 13
Contrition 16
The Lifting 17
You make us understand 20
Fishing boat 21
haiku 1 22
Morning coffee, Rouen 23
Mother and son 24
Time 25
Not sleeping 27
Solid people 29
Ormeau 30
Can you dance with me 32
A glass shattered 33
I twisted a rose for you 35
The Kingfisher 36
Leonard Cohen 37
As you hurry down the long hill 38
A walk in the forest 40
Winter came into the old house one night 41
The scent of flowers 42
The winding path 43
The bookcase 44
haiku 2 47
Silence 48
The Meaning of flowers 53
Standing on the edge 55
Passengers 56

Your own self   59
Accents   60
The man on the crossing   61
Making your place   63

Amoebae

when amoebae split
then
meet again
are they
we or me?

as you and I
became
we
in a simple
shape shift
of fate

Anthology

Poems crowded
musty in notebooks
loose pages
handwritten ink-faded
typed on an imperial portable
put away
at the back of a
wardrobe
in the cardboard suitcase...silently.

I lift each sheet and book confidentially
not willing that anyone
should see or hear the poems
as they goad me
into reckless remembering
and insinuate themselves
into a poet's conceit

II.

Now reading each verse
and free flowing, unpunctuated

I go back to the existence
and absurdity of places and lives:
the swish of soutanes
down polished corridors,
matins, lauds and vespers
scented with the trace
of incense and Sweet Afton

III.

Time of tides,
flowing in and out of the East Twin dock
the billowing smoke stacks
of the power station
reflected in the oil slicked channel
where the heaving
Maidstone docked
low in the water
under
heavy shackles and shame

Lapping the driftwood and waste
into verses of debris and death,
battles and bullets
closely typed with carbon copies

a new anthology

to be continued

IV.

Walking through unsafe streets
to warm bars
seething and singing
with promises of long nights
on cushion strewn floors in Stranmillis
red wine the curling, potent smoke;
long conversations with the girl
in the afghan coat
and knowing the meaning of life
and the incredible string band's
'koeeoaddi there'

Leafing pages on and on,
scanning the gentle words
written in the dreaming waves
of love and soaring passion

printed and poured over
scratched through - left to be
conjuring words with precision

intertwining conversations between
bigots and boors with poetic licence

V.

Moving from place to place
from year to year
hopeful and happily in love
and loving life and family
the children sincerely
promising and perfect

VI.

all the while
the world swirled outside
grasping and pulling
through the intricacies
of living and working
breathing, deeply

VII.

Now
parents dying and lifted up

finally, to be laid out in their silence
and words composed
and set aside for years
of always remembered

VIII.

Later walking in Rouen
over cobbled streets
standing in the Place Saint Marc
on a Sunday market morning
chez nous - completing a cycle
new dreams, new life, treasured

IX.

Over the Pyrenes through vineyards and forests,
footsore thankfully, on the Camino
tasting the essence of Rioja
and drinking in each step,
Castlle y Leon;
Galicia
each ascent and descent touching
with a sacred promise the closeness
that creates pilgrimage

X.

From the ream of pages,
poems written, challenged and refined
random phrases formed
rewritten, reformed,
lovingly inspired

created with vanity or struck out
casually with disdain
moments on moments
recalled and then rescinded
flooding and receding
half circled, half squared

sometimes broken
sometimes repaired
never destroyed
waiting to be read
aloud and heard

This is the Day

This is the day like all our days:

choose or don't choose

the joys and tribulations

of changing ways that appear

gust – sudden

like ribbons swept on the wind

now dancing

twisted

half-hidden

in sudden squalls and storms

or draped gently on the breeze

of auspicious fortune

wafting appealingly with ease

then sharply snapping

with the menace of unknown places

pleated with strange voices and designs

beckoning to unfamiliar ways

and unchartered spaces

So, take your care

of life's strange happenstance

stay softly still

to grasp

sudden wisps of happiness

before they whip away

until

another day like all our days

opens with more than was before

and stays for the shortest time.

So choose or don't choose

the way of venture or vision

or cast down your eyes

turn hopes and risk away

to suffer or delight in

small apathies and indifferences

or...

nothing at all

Lotissement

he walks up and down

bending, tending the rows

of green leaves and spreading stalks

his milieu;

hoeing eagerly with careless precision

stopping at the end of the lot

to pluck fruit

from a balanced

gently shuddering branch

as he moves;

treading, stooping

on stepping stones of old 'tin- cans'

with smiling respect

quietly strong

lifts his tipping full basket

to the fading deux chevaux

which waits at the edge of his allotment.

Ballyhornan

The beach edges onto the adventure of the sea
like a becoming certainty
a glance beyond, rests Gunn's Island,
ragged, rugged pastured, charmed;
out to where the cows' herd-swim
all tufted grass and virgin ribbons of sand,
a wading distance of the shore,
as gulls twirl and turn, dive and soar
squawk-shriek in the sky.
here, now, stepping beneath a cobalt sky;
this day on the dry white strand;
smithereens of shells, ground fine,
milled and washed through storms
and tides of a million waves;
a pristine beach; parchment white; rippled;
set down over ages;
for footprints to be made;
pictures to be drawn with driftwood pens.
far from land, the buoy-bell tolls
time to run, before evening falls
from the shore to the cottage on the road
back from being this small;
in the hugeness of the ocean sky;

in my small child's dream
at the end of a summer's day;
across the empty strand
across the pools and seaweeded rocks,
bare footed in the slanting summer twilight
from year to year,
a tide of memories
of this place
ebb and drift down
the depths of years
from now to before
always a summer evening,
always a gleaming salt sprayed shore
always Ballyhornan.

I was sad in my lacking to reach you

I was sad in my lacking to reach you

in your slow turning.

your eyes too dim for your journey

moving in small rhythms of farewells

that neither you nor I would acknowledge.

shifting and grasping parts of words

and making no sense nor sentences.

you're going now and I can't stop your leaving

you drift, in and out, back and never forward

but you left your quiet love

and your frantic caring

you left us our lives

and your smile

leaving and not knowing why nor when.

Finding my way

Finding my feet
in the darkness.
is it too strange and ridiculous?
in that deep night of the day when finding my feet, walking
across the top of Spain... 20 miles by that evening
to reach this place
of refuge and repose
with decent people and generous wine
where to place my step?
when my head is still in dreams,
my bladder punching above its weight
and the room's geography foreign
from the highest bunk
sealed in the zipped sleeping bag
careful of the narrow edge I rest on
among an exhaustion of travellers
stacked in bunks, row upon row
a dormitory of sleepers
weary from their trek
but happy to be on their way

the sounds of snores,
simpering, whistling like kettles
in small distorted harmonies
coughing, sighing in their phantom walking
striding champions
across mountain streams
towards their castles in Spain
but I am flaying silently to escape to the ground and
rush to the sound of the whispering cistern
so I peel out of the bag
kick off the jagged blanket
poise with legs swinging like pendulums.

14

a fall to the ground
is an option of gravity
but I take my time

in a hurried call-to-nature
sort of way
and drop silently to the bare boarded floor
finding my feet...finding my Way

Contrition

With a gasp of breath
I mouth to you a poem of regret
words of remorse

in your hesitant reply
you say nothing;

but with your finger poised
softly on your lips
like a silent benediction
your smile
makes
a prayer of forgiveness

The Lifting

My father carried me all the way

when I ran up to the road

to see him off the bus, coming from work.

and he lifted me over his shoulder

from my small child's running,

measuring strides all the way down South Parade,

between the aspen trees

carrying me with his bulging brief-case

balancing, our sure proud walk home.

Another time, before,

he lifted me, hot-fevered and sobbing

from the frost cold winter room at the top of our house,

to the perfumed-warm of their room below

and talk between them, soothed me to sleep

wrapped silent in the

wide folds of their bed.

he kept carrying me, right through those years;

when I was teenage confused, loosing chances;

he sat me down;

spoke straight, to lift me into reason

and, I chanced closeness to trust his word.

and he lifted me

holding me without condition;

marking my feeble pretensions with a pardon

for my embarrassed silences.

in death's desolation,

he sank, by my mother's leaving

then he wouldn't walk

and wouldn't think

or talk in straight sound reason

and couldn't lift me or he,

but struggled semi-sensible

groaning under a greater weight

than he had ever known;

and needed lifted himself;

that strong fine man, who lifted all our lives

and carried himself, proud and high

now wiped and wheeled about;

now pushed and pulled for far too long;

until he gave in and died.

Then we lifted him and raised him up,

to carry him slow and sad; in confused relief;

with silent measured stepping lifting, finally

and he didn't know.

You make us understand

you make us understand; you make us smile;
in our lives, competing with commotion;
you inspire certainty and trust; you make us wise

your difference makes our sameness tired;
expands our knowing with challenge and respect
you make us understand; you make us smile

your uniqueness makes us proud; enriches our lives
you have the care of all who know you
you inspire certainty and trust; you make us wise

ignore the flashing lights and roaring noise that defiles;
don't heed the fools that disrespect your lifestyle and
routine
you make us understand; you make us smile

this place, and all the ways you love are yours by right
all you feel and see in your mind, all your ways are kind
you inspire certainty and trust; you make us wise

don't fear the world that pretends and lies
makes their differing a dithering sham, a facade
you make us understand, you make us smile
you inspire certainty and trust; you make us wise

Fishing Boat

The fishing boat,
in tints of dusk and salt sea flecks
out in the as-far-as -can- be- seen sea distance
the fishing boat makes way
a flurry of foam in its wake
on the cobalt blue to opaque green,
dark-dark drowning depths
bottom trawling for whiting, cod and hake
where nets are ratchet-dropped into the evening swell
hauled creaking and straining in again
on fish scaled, oil-damp dieseled decks.

haiku 1

through the mist, leaves twirl
the world turns – and spins
dancing the night away

Morning coffee
Rouen

While you sleep deep and warm

I slip from the room into the morning rain

drag my wet feet to the corner café

exchanging 'bonjour' with the patron

sit by the window

scribble these early morning words

on a new page; in a new notebook

I sip black coffee;

the warmth, like your breath on my lips

I will make this a poem, for you,

and read it when you wake

Mother and son

on your doorstep
we felt the warm love of
mother and son
glimpsed the flame that
fires your soul and fuses you
with your baby and tempers you to strive and stride
longer and further than another one
who stays silently away, missing the years that
make the finest memories
but in your home, there is elation and
for good, always and happiness, always
for growing strong and singularly intent to succeed
alone but never lonely; living your life; making your story
you, our daughter, as great as only a woman can be.

Time

Time slips, drips and flows into a pool...
wider and deeper, filled, year by year... with
memories, recalled
in quick rhythms ...to thrill and stir the
senses;
the reasons we live and the purpose we love...
floating on tides, ebbing...then surging;
of passion and expressions of forever...

now... in the quiet,
hard times, dark words and clouded minds
submerge to depths to be confined but never
drowned
now...precious times emerge
...light,
incandescent...
shimmering across the surface ripples...
and time slips, leaks, into the pool of memory
deeper... day by day;
constancy and visceral attachment
still ... making time precious for day by day ...
filling the pool to brimming...with the hours we live...
still to be remembered...
as sudden waves...across the stilled surface...
broken, by quick shards of sadness...
disturbing composure, but still...
precious times keeps flowing,
on tides, swirls and instants
like pebbles thrown into the pool,

making the circles that run out and out,
to the edge
to overflow into memories
deeper by each year
caught by the glistening hooks
that snag the joy of
sudden touch
a glance
a certain scent
the words of a poem
so… time slips, drips and flows into a pool
of memories
wider and deeper
year by year;
precious time

Not sleeping

I didn't sleep…
it's complicated
there is so much
for which to be awake
warm words
mummering softly
on your slumbering lips
the dawn forming
between now and morning
slipping through the part drawn curtains
small dreams, only begun…
then melting into
a nebulous otherness
then…
flickering… 'just there' …
just beyond a silent touch,
memories emerge
then fade, secretly away…
until
the sneaking mutter of unease
makes 'awake in the night '
dreadful and disquieting…

rattles of worry

discordant, tangled and habitual

strung out like beads

on the edge of certainty

'til… in the forming stillness

sleep seeps and spins like

prayers whirring on wheels

so fine filigreed, in gold,

as slumbers should be

yearning to tumble in and down

deep, dark and rest

bathing in waves', tired - heavy

timed out and exhausted

with exhaustion

wearied, with squinted eyes and yawning mouth…

time to

close down, close eyes, close the book

and say goodnight… even as late

as in this pulsing morning's light

I didn't sleep…

it's complicated

Solid people

rhyming non sequitur
and here's the thing;
and did you know?
have you heard?
going on about the hunt for any other
another; anyone
who does not share blood
anyone who falters or flinches
in the muddle fuddle of their lives
in their troubled
pained confusion of living
true or without truth
but good enough
to spread thickly and trickily;

as a mbeal beag agus bocht

good titbit or full repeat and applaud;
snigger and giggle like farts
rhymers and tellers of tales
savouring debt, death and destruction,
pregnancy, abortion, sex and suicide
of who else but anybody to keep the evil eye
away from themselves;
cast it quickly and often on those
who run out into the open jaws of bigots and bores,
gombeens and brats
a station above their aspirations
stabbing deeper and silently
close to the heart of their being
with as much insight
as can gather in the eye of a needle
and be pulled through in a stitch of time
by tricksters in their mindless frenzy
ever so poor mouths

Ormeau

Ormeau means
young elm – in French
some say
'elm by the water'
Orme and eau – you see, orm eau:
I choose to know they're wrong
I favour 'young elm'.
Ormeau
my home in the city

I ran through my childhood
on the Ormeau road,
in the park
sometimes in and out
of the Ormeau bakery shop
fetching live yeast
wrapped in a twist of paper
for my mother – occasionally - to make bread
a penny farthing
that's all it cost

the smell of fresh baked bread
through the kitchen, in the house
infused outside with the hot crust essence of the
bakery
it laid warmth on the air
a comfort distilled
floating
all the way down
the road

as far as the bridge
to the lagan

then the slow traces
emerge sluggishly
a throat catching whiff
close and equally familiar
coke and sulphur
sharp and acrid
suffusing the air as its own
contrived in the gasometers
moving imperceptibly and huge
a giant's pot of steaming fume
telescoping down
pushing gas through snaking pipes
hissing across the city

to street lamps
to cook breakfasts and dinners
putt- popping of gas fires
firing up the immensity of ovens in the bakery
naked flamed; the hot extracted air laden with
promise of a share of bread
from the shop
an unwrapped plain loaf

excavated and half eaten
between the bakery and home
running through a childhood
in Ormeau
a young elm growing

Can you dance with me?

can you dance with me?
kick your shoes out of sight
sashay round the floor
in abandon and delight

or will you move with me?
face to face
arms straight strained
never moving, stooped in fright

will you sing with me?
loud and unrestrained
raising the roof
proud and unashamed
or will you chant with me
a mournful dirge
voiced sad and low

with no ending and no surge

will you talk with me?
close as breathing
tête-à-tête you to me
almost touching, replete with sudden feeling

or will you speak to me?
in murmured sighs and distraction
wishing for the night to fall

A glass shattered

a glass shattered on the tiled terrace
in a scattering of pieces
then you - light footed
stepped on a shard
pierced your gentle foot
as you walked unknowing
leaving blood blots
on each terrazzo square
until you grimaced- cried
with the sharp sudden pain
and your friends
gathered anxious- inquisitive round
and the sun in your face waned to pale
you feint-folded
and I carried you into the house
caring that you were still my child

then those who thought they knew
mechanically lifted your still bleeding foot
and engineered to operate with tweezers
but gave up the project
of surgical searching and prodding

the very sole of your foot

but the tiny spear remained

buried straight, hidden

until anxious-proud

I moved forward and with nervous purpose

wiped away the blood and found the searing splinter

and pulled it deftly out and away

proud to be he who eased his daughter's pain

quietly content, being your father.

I twisted a rose for you

I twisted a rose from the briar last night
it was spiral stemmed and complicated in its way

I pulled it down from the thorned briar
and cut my hand to the bone

I left that flower to die on the ground
rather than give to you; or anyone

my blood dripped slowly on the bruised flower
in turn the rose bled from its petals

The kingfisher

on an overhanging branch
the kingfisher attends the morning stream
flowing below in a seamless whisper
fixed eyed as in a dream

between slow deep and sudden shallow
the shimmer sequined bird, content
remains perched and balanced;
as the river drifts its way with calm intent

the kingfisher, alert, waits expectant
for a ripple, or slightest glimpse
now she dives, in a burst of silken hues
orange, cyan and blue, into the flow

spearing and lifting a small fish, perfectly
from the burnished pool
to strike against the bough,
swallow then deploys again purposefully

on an overhanging branch
the kingfisher attends the morning stream
flowing below in a seamless whisper
fixed eyed as in a dream

I am here watching
with concern for its ending
too suddenly

Leonard Cohen

A man in his muse from a secret yeshiva
composing poems quick and ponderous
transformed to songs with aplomb and chutzpah
lilts and lifts over dark sombre voice
insinuating our lives, mood of candle light
reflecting hue of wine and loose strung guitars
discrete behind flaking doors of smoky city nights
words of love obtuse and impossible
probable when the air thinned and angels sang
a thousand kisses deep:
the holy, the sacred subtly divine;
crafted, ominous, famous dark blue raincoat
then in in New York, before you took Manhattan
with Jane, Marianne, Joni and Suzanne,
blue and mesmerising, their silken hair
flowing kaftans, in your secret life
songs and verses, faceted with elusive incensed words
now a zen master
intoning deep-throated chant in the monastery
away from any sisters of mercy;
away from the chelsea hotel or boogie street
elegant of mood, lighter of life
now you want it darker
swirling and moving to the end of love
dancing to the end of time.

As you hurry down the long hill

I sat by the river Orb
in Languedoc;
sat in the early morning sun, San Miguel de Salinas;
sat by the sodden green in my garden in Tyrone
I start these words:
as you hurry down the long hill from Boulingran
to the Place Saint Marc in Rouen
as you do most days
your back pack holds your writing tools
Moleskine notebook
bulging with your words –songs – poems
your stories
scattered words and moments - your thoughts
bon mots – recklessly sacred to your purpose
precisely profane and existential
carefully arrowed to their target
cutting into the wholesome
and fucking orthodoxy
to shock the predictably shockable
imploding hypocrisy and pretence to a
simpering whisper
and still, you hold on to your purposeful entrancing dream
forging truths, blow by blow,
from the melting red hot lexicon of your experience
forming a clear definite voice
telling your freedom in pages and books
rattling doubts to promise of enchantment
wielding your pen as a palette knife
to lay the paintwords thick with intent
drawing careful figures and sentient shapes
from your latent strength – that you may not discern.
then as you walk down the hill
from Boulingran to the grande marché

open your clenched hand as you opened your fist
the night you were born
and remember the words I wrote
hold on to your dream and let not those
who know little,
or nothing
dare to doubt you'
that you can craft and weave that dream
perfectly into your caring senses
let your words and your soul have their raison d'etre

I sit here or there
you stride down the hill
into the heart of Rouen or anywhere
goading the world to make sense
and you fear what you fear
I shrink from writing this
lest it is fraudulent;
or I vicariously intrude on your freedom.

A walk in the forest

walking in the deep forest in whispered glades
by moss moist carpets under bifurcated trees
tangled over the trails that keep the imprint of steps
in earth and mud from beyond past times
beside memories of lakes, where reflections
once rippled beyond imagining
holding the sounds and murmurings
we walk still to our purpose
heeding the sounds of trees and birds calling
listening to each other's words and instances
making our own curious twists and turns
through glades that make peace in silent being
in the healing of a smile;
the understanding of a hand touch-brushed
softly with gentle haste as we walk back
to where we were through the tease of spring;
the flourish of summer;
the vacancy of autumn;
the absolution of winter;
pardoning the slightest breeze
that might intrude
in these wooded cloisters
set down for times ahead,
our history of moments
to be covered and shrouded, hidden,
encased in humus draped in ferns
until unearthed
by distant future pilgrims
walking alone
or together
making their stanza for this poem

Winter came into the old house one night

Winter came into the old house one night
sudden, callous, flickering the lights
running and tripping across the slates
thundering in the chimneys rattling a gate

winter came into the old house last night
blowing, shrilling like a whale in flight
soaking and chilling cracking window panes
blustering and cackling, gurgling through the drains

winter came into the old house tonight
gathered close together in the fast firelight
we spoke softly of life and laughed at the squall
letting winter stream above and beyond us all

The Scent of Flowers

In the sunlit
morning room
yes
the scent of flowers
atomized from the blooms
still garden fresh
unseen, yet
a potent evocation
of before and always
the traces of spring
a diaphanous veil
draped over the room
yes, the scent of flowers

The winding path

we travelled on a winding path
of dust to mud with open hearts
up into the mountains of Leon on through
to *Galaxia*
on breathless slopes and gasping
rugged ways
we made good time
met good people
and promised to meet
for octopus or cabbage soup
and a fine Gallaecian wine.

The bookcase

the bookcase stands - beeswax polished;

the smell of sun-baked oak
 caught in the wood grain
since it was made
with the carefulness of an apprentice.

built piece by piece;
dovetailed and planed into an object of strength
that furnished our childhood dreams
of places and nations' mystical notions;
stories and tales of before,
since and future;
mystery of beyond the stars;
gazing through the fragile glass doors;
to wonder at the paperbacks,
leather and cloth spines
that were guarded and pleasing to our parents;
but not to be opened by prying small fingers;
the brass key locking out the inquisitive,
unready for grown up reading;
the orange penguins,

pale blue pelicans;
 the yellow and red left book club;
Homage to Catalonia;
The Road To Wigan Pier
stacked and neatly rowed,
aligned and tightly organised
into this four-shelf library,
mirroring times and lives of a family;
later when the rites of reading emerged;
 the glass doors opened,
 to fables and tales to be explored;
 the touch and smell of paper, ink and binding glue;
 books to sooth the fever of needing to know;
 to channel angst
describe how complex
 and dangerous is the world;
seeking and reading,
turning pages, never forgotten;
kept and talked of how
the bookcase was their wedding present
in april nineteen thirty-nine
now standing in my hall way;
the lines of books behind glass doors,
probed by grandchildren
their prying fingers seeking the brass key;

the books changed;

some dispersed, lent and lost;

some remain precious and fragile;

a paper trail to my family past

replaced by our books,

that my children sought out and leafed

on wet days of playing school or building towers;

the bookcase stands beeswax polished.

haiku 2

in the glaring sun
hungry stork chicks clatter beaks
the ring of church bells

Silence

silence surrounds

it gathers into itself

silence endures calmly above us all

it is the just before

silence is

on the very edge of joy

it is on the margin of desolation

silence is

contemplating a blank page

it is the expectation of inspiration

silence is

between the notes of music

it is between the wondering

and the beginning

it is the prelude to the dawn chorus

silence is

the quiet still voice

that waits

it is fragile as a frozen leaf

it is an autumn breath

silence is

both blissful

and brutal

it is the calm

confronting contempt

it is the truth

that never

speaks

silence is

the before;

the after

the above,

the beneath

it is the moment before a baby's first cry

it clasps the air

of a final breath

silence is

carrying a sleeping child

it is the stillness

that can make wrongs right

it is the instant before

decision

silence is the

chilled awareness

of fear

silence is

the downcast eyes of

humiliation

it is the long lonely walk

of a woman

just going home

silence is

the gagged mouth of

rebellion

it is the taped closed lips of

protest

it is the walking away from

brutality

it is the tears flowing in

defeat

silence is

expectation

it is the moments between

the chimes of a clock

between a harsh word and

shame

silence is passion in a

smile

it is the deepest

trust

that grows with

years

sometimes

it is all there is

The meaning of flowers

Flowers

in single stems

bouquets,

sprays and posies

with vivid hues

and pungent scents

to say:

sorry...

...forgive me

I'm not with you...

...but I miss you

I love you

Flowers in a spontaneous cluster

Say:

...I'm thinking of you today

In my own way...

in a vase, solidly

when they are given

to say:

Better late than never…

…I want to ease your pain

Brighten your day…

…well done

…Bientot.

Standing on the edge

I am standing on the edge
of a terrible reality
you are there, unknowing
eyes closed
without movement
comatose
not in the world
the machinery hisses and pumps
syringes drive the vital substance to keep you here
the ventilator distorts and obscures your face
but still I know you
placing my hand on your head
know and whisper
this is not how it's supposed to be
father to son
I stay to see your eyes open

but for so long, so long
they do not...
as I leave the room
I realise
I know nothing of the sequences and balances of life
but so much more
of love and pain

Passengers

I slide my bus pass on the pad
tell the driver 'not a bad day'.
sidle my way between the seats.
people settled for the journey:
one: silent, absorbed in quiet concerns;
another or two: i suppose, happy,
indifferent and inscrutably sad:
going to college – late for class; trembling into an
outpatient's cubicle to see what's to be seen;
going, shopping, hopping between stops and starts.
going to sit by a hospital bed
going to the grave of an unknown relative;
to a visit in prison -the first time ever
a therapist's chair;
to relax as deep as childhood memories stay
to sit, to watch; to listen.
making a journey in hope and cautious care
of failing that only comes with despair and silvering hair.
a good time to gossip but careful who is sitting near – can
overhear;
with glances – left right speak; right- left speak;

check quick backward glance at the most
just keep this to yourself look so careful,
squeaking past an 'artic'
perhaps on its way to the docks in belfast
onwards then, perhaps to iceland
each passenger:
thinking their way out of or into trouble;
writing a verse in their head propped against the window;
rocking in a transit rhythm;
making their peace with an iphone;
watching football on a stream;

predicting replies;
rehearsing the words that will make falling in love real and
forever.
other people doze for lack of sleep
from last night's excesses of booze, sex or sadness.
stopping at lough road, half- way,
a man with a pony tail flicks and dances down the bus
speaks to the driver, then quick steps off
and lifts his luggage from the boot:
i wonder- is he waiting for the bus to Dublin

        . . . it doesn't come this route

        . . . he looks concerned and foreign-as we whine
        away

        . . . people at the front seats are perturbed for his
        being, but not his leaving

        . . . examine his deportment and speak of him and
        his like causing queues at the doctors and running
        down the neighbourhood

        . . . and the how large suitcases speak of
        permanence and invasion

the rest of us in uneasy shame and solidarity, stay on,
towards Belfast to eat and drink;
to work, study, meet and greet;
to arrive early or fashionably late;
relaxed; nervous as the silence of a crowd,
road-gazing abandoned and alone.
a woman in an aisle seat,
up- ends a giant bag of crisps,
rattles the last of them down her ample throat
smoothing her hair with salt and vinegared fingers.
still rolling, squeaking, suspended along,
passing cars with drivers oblivious to our presence up here,
peering down from this translink tardis and what we see:

the texting; onehanded resting;

gesticulating hands free; coffee cup drinking;

sandwich munching; passenger trolling.

the blue velour seats carpeted rows like a moving cinema.
movies on the road rolling, reeling.
close to Belfast the phone calls in-pour like audible
dominos,
falling along the seatrows . . .

> *'hello, I'm on the bus; I'll see you later. . .'*
> *'I'm on the bus, I can't wait. . .'*
> *'yea! where will you wait for me. . .'*
> *'I'm on the bus into the Europa. . .'*
> *'no, not the hotel, the bus station. . .'*
> *'glengall street over the boyne bridge. . .'*
> *'still on the bus, on our way in. . .'*
> *'I'm on the bus, arriving soon . . . how will I know*
> *you?'*

an almost, wish i wasn't here silence of the crowd
a quiet mumble; a simper; a hush
activity increases in the journey-end bustle
the aftershock amid coat putting on
scarf untwining; shoes remembered; bags zipped and
fastened
the bus slides into the docking bay
the passenger commune toddle, stride and dribble
off the mother craft
dispersing in spurts and hurries
into the rush of the commute.

Your own self

you always fill us
with your smile
in your rushing through
the joy of life
with urgent speed
 a quiet constancy of purpose
hanging your clothes on the floor
irritating
but in retrospect
pleases as a memory because
you have more
important business
to busy you
things that excite
your growing
to be your own self

Accents

my mother's voice
was the soft hug of a Mersey dawn
with a gentle inflection
on her word endings
brought from
Woolton village
and spoken with ease,
yielding as a mist,
gliding up to the bows
of the morning boat into the Mersey

The man on the crossing

the man on the crossing
carries the weight.
a newspaper under each arm
one for the local woes and wows
the hatches, dispatches and police catches.

the other of a wider world
of floods, wars; burning; earth shaking;
people haters; child snatches.

he hesitates, examines his shoes and stops,
turns his head to the church,
immovable on the hill;
shifts and hobbles back across the road

like beads of sacred oil,
tears appear on his cheek
but he continues to process;
crooked like a pilgrim
under the weight of pain

shuffling in a slow dance;

to a dirge, unsung but plain
up to the church
silently and unobserved

on his shallow breath
a blessing intoned
to his own purpose

he enters the porch and moves
like a phantom to the nave
to lay prostrate on cold marble steps
a riposte to all that
is wrong and duplicitous
quietly now in dignity
a solitary liberation.

Making your place

from the time you
were born
our first daughter
making your place

you understood
the meaning of your name
'renowned warrior'

making your mind up
early
to be strong
as your instinct
to be clear to be sure
making your mind up
making your place

at three
on a summers holiday
cossetted in your cardigan
on the sun-bathed beach
determined
not to comply
until sandcastles and sea
drew you into play
with your brother
and us
happily
making your place
making your mind up

and on that journey
to where you are

trusted and tested
making your place
in your own true life

an attentive
essential person
mother
your children
learning from your closeness
growing
making your place

as you guide them
with careful words
resolve
with clear sight
making their place

we know
the daughter
who loves
gives care and concern

all the while
transforming challenge
and grasping
prospects
making your mind up

now with your family
making your life
keeping faith
with tenacity
making your mind up

Acknowledgements

The poem *'The Lifting'* was broadcast on RTE's Sunday Miscellany, June 18, 2006.

The poems: *'Winter came into the old house one night'; 'Can you dance with me?'*, and *'Leonard Cohen'* appeared in *'Reflections', Poetry and Prose'* by Burnavon Writers, 2019.

'The Meaning of Flowers' and *'The Scent of Flowers'* were first published in *'Flowers...in paint and verse'* by Geoffrey Bye & Michael May, 2022.

CPSIA information can be obtained
at www.ICGtesting.com
Printed in the USA
BVHW052326300123
657507BV00012B/155